Published by: **Sourcebooks, Inc.**
P.O. Box 372, Naperville, Illinois, 60566
(708) 961-3900
FAX: (708) 961-2168

Editorial: Todd Stocke
Cover Design: Wayne Johnson
Interior Design: Wayne Johnson, Sourcebooks, Inc.
Production: Corey Dean

ISBN: 1-57071-034-1

Printed and bound in the United States of America.
10 9 8 7 6 5 4 3 2 1

RANDOM ACTS

A KINDNESS JOURNAL

**From the bestselling book by
the Editors of Conari Press**

Sourcebooks, Inc.
Naperville, IL

"Fear grows out of the things we think; it lives in our minds. Compassion grows out of the things we are, and lives in our hearts."

—Barbara Garrison

Praise the work or attitude of a person you work with to someone else in the office in a time, place, and manner that is outside of all office politics.

"The quality of mercy
is not strained;
it dropeth as the gentle rain
from heaven;
upon the place beneath;
it is twice blessed;
it blesseth him that giveth
and him that takes."

— William Shakespeare

"...loving and being loved is the one true human vocation."

—Daphne Rose Kingma

'In giving love, you yourself will understand that we are held in the web of life—and delivered to our divine humanity—by the random acts of kindness, the love, that we give and receive.'

—Daphne Rose Kingma

Get your children to go through their toys and put aside those they want to donate to children who are less fortunate.

_____

_____

_____

_____

_____

_____

_____

_____

'Once you begin to acknowledge random acts of
kindness —both the ones you have received and the ones you have given—
you can no longer believe that what you do does not matter.'

—Dawna Markova

Order a mail-order gift, anonymously, for a
friend or someone at work who needs to be cheered up.

"Today, see if you can stretch your heart and expand your love so that it touches not only those to whom you can give it easily, but also to those who need it so much."

—Daphne Rose Kingma

"The purpose of life is a
life of purpose."
—Robert Byrne

'Kind words can be short and easy to speak
but their echoes are truly endless.'

— Mother Teresa

Ask an older person to tell you a story about his or her youth, such as what her favorite song was and why, or how he met his spouse.

17

'A knowledge of the path cannot be substituted
for putting one foot in front of the other.'
—M. C. Richards

Make a list of things to do to bring more kindness into the world and have a friend make a list. Exchange lists and do one item per day for a month.

"Life is short and we have never too much time for gladdening the hearts of those who are travelling the dark journey with us. Oh be swift to love, make haste to be kind."

—Henri Frederick Amiel

"It is possible to decrease the suffering
in the world by adding to the joy. It
is possible to add light rather than
trying to destroy the darkness."

—Dawna Markova

'A hundred times every day I remind myself that my inner and outer life depends on the labors of other men, living and dead, and that I must exert myself in order to give in the measure as I have received and am still receiving.'

—Albert Einstein

Offer to help people who could use the assistance to cross streets—seniors, the blind, small children...

'It is one of the most beautiful compensations of life that no man can sincerely try to help another without helping himself.'

— Ralph Waldo Emerson

Next time you go to the ice cream parlor, pay for a few free cones to be given to the next kids to come in.

"The great, dominant, all controlling fact of this life is the innate bias of the human spirit, not towards evil, as the theologists tell us, but towards good."

—William Archer

"It is good to have an end to journey
toward; but it is the journey that
matters in the end."

—Ursula K. LeGuin

'We cannot live only for ourselves.
A thousand fibers connect us with our fellow men;
and among those fibers, as sympathetic threads, our actions
run as causes, and they come back to us as effects.'
—Herman Melville

Plant a tree in your neighborhood.

'Life is no 'brief candle' to me. It is a sort of splendid torch which I have got hold of for a moment, and I want to make it burn as brightly as possible before handing it on to future generations.'

—George Bernard Shaw

Talk to people at work about one of your random acts of kindness and ask what one of theirs is. Disclosure stimulates us to do more by emphasizing the pleasure of giving with no strings attached.

"I keep my ideals, because in spite of everything I still believe that people are really good at heart."

                    –Anne Frank

"Whenever you are to do a thing, though it can never be known but to yourself, ask yourself how you would act were all the world looking at you and act accordingly."

—Thomas Jefferson

`I am of the opinion that my life belongs
to the community and as long as I live, it is my privilege
to do for it whatever I can.'

—George Bernard Shaw

Write a note to the boss of someone who has helped you, thanking him or her for having such a great employee.

"Put your heart, mind, intellect and soul even
to your smallest acts. This is the secret of success."

—Swami Sivananda

Laugh out loud often and share your smile generously.

"Kindness is more important than wisdom, and the recognition of this is the beginning of wisdom."

—Theodore Isaac Rubin

"Our deeds determine us, as much as we determine our deeds."

—George Eliot

'Some day after we have mastered the winds, the waves, the tides and gravity we shall harness the energies of love. Then, for the second time in the history of the world, man will have discovered fire.'

—Teilhard de Chardin

Organize your friends and workmates to gather their old clothes and give them to homeless people.

49

'Living the truth in your heart without compromise brings kindness into the world. Attempts at kindness that compromise your heart cause only sadness.'

—Anonymous 18th century monk

As you go about your day,
why not pick up the trash you find on the sidewalk?

51

"By the accident of fortune a man may rule the world for a time, but by virtue of love and kindness he may rule the world forever."

—Lao-Tse

"We do not remember days, we remember moments."

—Casare Pavese

"I don't know what your destiny will be,
but one thing I do know: the only ones among you who will
be really happy are those who have sought and found how to serve."
—Albert Schweitzer

Give another driver your parking spot.

57

"We may have all come on different ships,
but we're in the same boat now."
— Martin Luther King, Jr.

Visit a neighbor with a
bouquet of flowers for no reason at all.

"To become the perpetrator of random acts of kindness. . . means you have moved beyond the limits of your daily human condition to touch wings with the divine."
—Daphne Rose Kingma

"Charity is the bone shared with the dog when you are just as hungry as the dog."

—Jack London

"Tenderness and kindness are not signs of weakness
and despair but manifestations of strength and resolution."
—Kahlil Gibran

Hold a random acts of kindness party where everyone tells the stories of kindnesses in their life.

'Each small task of everyday life is part of
the total harmony of the universe.'
—St. Theresa of Lisieux

Make an anonymous donation to some local charity that is actively helping people—feeding the homeless, providing foster care for children, and so on.

"Kindness is tenderness,
kindness is love, perhaps
greater than love. . . kindness
is goodwill, kindness says
'I want you to be happy.'"

—Randolph Ray

"Wherever there is a human being
there is an opportunity for kindness."
—Seneca

'If someone comes to you asking for help, do
not say in refusal, 'Trust in God, HE will help.' Rather,
act as if there were no God, and no one to help except you.'
—Zaddik

Send a letter to a teacher you once had letting her know about the difference she made in your life.

"The course of human history is determined,
not by what happens in the skies, but by what takes place in our hearts."
—Sir Arthur Keith

Buy a big box of donuts or chocolates for the office next to yours. Or the kids who hang out on the street corner. Or the UPS person or the mail carrier.

"My religion is very simple.
My religion is kindness."
—The Dalai Lama

"To receive everything, one must open one's hands and give."

—Taisen Deshimaru

'Let us not be satisfied with just giving money.
Money is not enough, money can be got, but they need your hearts
to love them. So, spread your love everywhere you go.'
— Mother Teresa

Walk around with an instamatic
camera and take people's pictures and give them to them.

"For, in enacting these beautiful, spontaneous, wholly gratuitous goodnesses, you transform not only the world, but yourself."
—Daphne Rose Kingma

Spend a week just being aware
of things in nature that befriend you.

"If you bring forth what is inside of you, what you bring forth will save you. If you don't bring forth what is inside of you, what you don't bring forth will destroy."

—Jesus

"The heart that breaks open can
contain the whole universe."

—Joanna Macy

"A gift consists not in what is done or given, but in the intention of the giver or doer."

—Seneca

Let the person behind you in line at the grocery store go ahead of you.

'Our brightest blazes of gladness are
commonly kindled by unexpected sparks.'
—Dr. Johnson

Make a dedication on your local radio station to all those people who smiled at strangers today.

"Let us not be justices of the peace, but angels of peace."
—St. Theresa of Lisieux

"Give help rather than advice."

—Luc de Vauvenargues

"Do every act of your life as if it were your last."
— Marcus Aurelius

Slip a $20 bill into the
pocketbook of a needy friend (or stranger).

'If there is any kindness I can show, or any
good thing I can do to any fellow being, let me do it now,
and not deter or neglect it, as I shall not pass this way again.'
—William Penn

If there is a garden you pass frequently and enjoy, stop by one day and leave a note letting the occupants know how much pleasure their garden gives you.

"The best portions of a
good man's life,
His little, nameless,
unremembered acts,
Of kindness and love."

—William Wordsworth

"The principle of self-cultivation
consists in nothing but trying to look
for the lost heart."

—Mencius

'Complete possession is proved only by giving.
All you are unable to give possesses you.'
—Andre Gide

Yes, it's a drag, but why not put your shopping cart back in its appointed place in the parking lot?

'. . .practice random acts of kindness, so that
which came to you as seed will be passed on to the next as blossom,
and that which came to you as blossom will go on as fruit.'

—Dawna Markova

Spend half an hour in a hospital emergency room and do one random act of kindness that presents itself.

"Five things constitute perfect virtue: gravity, magnanimity, earnestness, sincerity and kindness."

—Confucius

"What wisdom can you find that is greater than kindness?"

—Jean Jaques Rousseau

'We are trained to believe that we don't matter
and that we cannot make a difference. But we can.'
—Dawna Markova

Send a fax to someone you don't know and start a random acts of kindness chain fax letter.

'This only is charity, to do all, all that we can.'
—John Donne

114

If you know someone who is going through a bad day or a difficult time in life, make it better by doing something—anything—to let him or her know that someone cares... and don't let on who did it.

115

"The ideals which have lighted my way, and time after time have given me new courage to face life cheerfully, have been Kindness, Beauty, and Truth."

—Albert Einstein

"It is better to give and receive."

—Bernard Gunther

... you must also create space in your life
for the expression of gratitude. What has sustained your soul?
What has inspired you to hold on when all else was pulling you
over a cliff?'

—Dawna Markova

Say "thank you" to someone who helps you and really mean it. You might want to look into his *eyes*, smile, and, if he is wearing a name tag, say his name as well.

"Through our willingness to help others we can
learn to be happy rather than depressed."

—Gerald Jampolsky

Go to an AIDS hospice or
hospital ward and see what you can do for one person.

"If you help others, you will
be helped, perhaps tomorrow,
perhaps in one hundred years,
but you will be helped.
Nature must pay off the
debt . . . . It is a mathematical
law and all life is
mathematics."

—Gurdjieff

"Love is not getting, but giving."
—Henry Van Dyke

'What you deny to others will be denied to you,
for the plain reason that you are always legislating for yourself;
all your words and actions define the world you want to live in.'
—Thaddeus Golas

If someone in your neighborhood leaves on a trip and forgets to stop the newspaper, pick them up and put them in a safe out-of-view spot.

'Little kindnesses . . . will broaden your heart, and slowly you will habituate yourself to helping your fellow man in many ways.'

—Zaddik

Write a letter of appreciation to that which in nature has been a safe place for you.

"If you stop to be kind, you must swerve often from your path."

—Mary Webb

"He alone is great who turns the voice of the wind into a song made sweeter by his own loving."

—Kahlil Gibran

"The beginning and end of Torah is performing acts of loving kindness."

—The Talmud

If you have any artistic abilities, buy a bag full of art supplies and take it and yourself out to a playground or recreation center in a poor neighborhood and go to it.

'Keep on sowing your seed, for you never know
which will grow—perhaps it all will'
—Ecclesiastes

For one week, act on every single thought of generosity that arises spontaneously in your heart and notice what happens as a consequence.

"It is in the shelter of each
other that the people live."

—Irish Proverb

"Give light, and the darkness will
disappear of itself."

—Erasmus

'I believe that man will not merely endure; he will prevail. He is immortal, not because he alone among the creatures has an inexhaustible voice, but because he has a soul, a spirit capable of kindness and compassion.'

—William Faulkner

Find someone you've been close to and sit back to back with her. For a few minutes disclose the random acts of kindness she has done for you while she just listens. Then switch and listen to the wonderful things you have done.

145

'Twas a thief said the last word to Christ.
Christ took the kindness and forgave the theft.'
—Robert Browning

The next time someone speaks to you, listen deeply without expecting anything.

"Shall we make a new rule of life from tonight: always to try to be a little kinder than is necessary."

—Sir James M. Barrie

"Our lives are fed by kind words and gracious behavior."

—Ed Hays

'Experience praises the most happy the one
who made the most people happy.'
—Karl Marx

152

Open the phone book and select
a name at random and send that person a greeting card.

'...Do not believe what your teacher tells you merely out of respect for the teacher. But whatsoever, after due examination and analysis, you find to be kind, conducive to the good, the benefit, the welfare of all beings –that doctrine believe and cling to, and take it as your guide.'

—Buddha

Take the opportunity in conversation with friends to tell them about kindness you have experienced and ask about their experiences. Just talking about acts of kindness brings them alive in the world.

"...it is in giving oneself that one receives; it is forgetting oneself that one is found; it is in pardoning that one obtains pardon."

—St. Francis of Assisi